FAVORITE
BASEBALL
★ TEAMS ★

ST. LOUIS
CARDINALS

BY K.C. KELLEY

The Child's World

Published by The Child's World®
1980 Lookout Drive • Mankato, MN 56003-1705
800-599-READ • www.childsworld.com

ACKNOWLEDGMENTS
The Child's World®: Mary Berendes,
      Publishing Director
The Design Lab: Kathleen Petelinsek, Design
Shoreline Publishing Group, LLC: James
      Buckley Jr., Production Director

PHOTOS
Cover: Focus on Baseball
Interior: All photos by Focus on Baseball except:
AP/Wide World: 5, 9, 17, 22 inset, 25 bottom left,
26 inset; Getty Images: 18, 22 main

LIBRARY OF CONGRESS
CATALOGING-IN-PUBLICATION DATA
Kelley, K. C.
   St. Louis Cardinals / by K.C. Kelley.
      p. cm. — (Favorite baseball teams)
   Includes index.
   ISBN 978-1-60253-382-0 (library bound : alk. paper)
   1. St. Louis Cardinals (Baseball team)—History—
Juvenile literature. I. Title. II. Series.
   GV875.S74K45 2010
   796.357'640977866—dc22   2009039453

Printed in the United States of America
Mankato, Minnesota
November 2009
F11460

On the cover: Albert Pujols, First Base

CONTENTS

Go, Cardinals!

In the history of baseball, only one team has been more successful than the St. Louis Cardinals. Packed with stars and cheered by **loyal** fans, the Cardinals have won 10 **World Series**. That's second only to the New York Yankees' 26 titles. Cardinals fans have enjoyed lots of great seasons watching their team. Let's meet the Cardinals!

Cardinals star Albert Pujols met President Barack Obama at the ▶ 2009 **All-Star Game**. The game was played in St. Louis.

Who Are the Cardinals?

The St. Louis Cardinals are a team in baseball's National League (N.L.). The N.L. joins with the American League to form Major League Baseball. The Cardinals play in the Central Division of the N.L. The division winners get to play in the league playoffs. The playoff winners from the two leagues face off in the World Series. The Cardinals have won 10 World Series championships.

◀ Albert Pujols shows why he is one of the best hitters in baseball.

Where They Came From

A team called the St. Louis Browns played in a league in the 1800s. It was called the American Association. That team joined the National League in 1892. In 1899, they changed their name to the Perfectos. Then, in 1900, they became the Cardinals. That's the team that continues to play in St. Louis today. The Cardinals are one of the oldest Major League teams. They won their first World Series in 1926. They won their most recent Series in 2006.

Lou Brock, Julian Javier, and Bob Gibson celebrated after the Cardinals ▶
won the 1967 World Series.

Who They Play

The St. Louis Cardinals play 162 games each season. That includes about 15 games against the other teams in their division, the N.L. Central. The Cardinals have won seven N.L. Central championships. The other Central teams are the Chicago Cubs, the Cincinnati Reds, the Houston Astros, the Milwaukee Brewers, and the Pittsburgh Pirates. The Cardinals and the Cubs are big **rivals**. Their games always get the fans charged up! The Cardinals also play some teams from the American League. Their A.L. **opponents** change every year.

◄ Here's action from an N.L. Central game between the Cardinals and the Pittsburgh Pirates.

11

Where They Play

In 2006, the Cardinals moved into a brand-new ballpark. Like their old home, it was called Busch Stadium. It was easy to find, too. The new stadium was built right next door to the old one! Fans sitting behind **home plate** can enjoy a view of the St. Louis Arch. This huge, steel arch is a world-famous landmark.

The St. Louis Arch rises over the right field wall of Busch Stadium. Behind ▶ left field, fans can see the green-topped state capitol building.

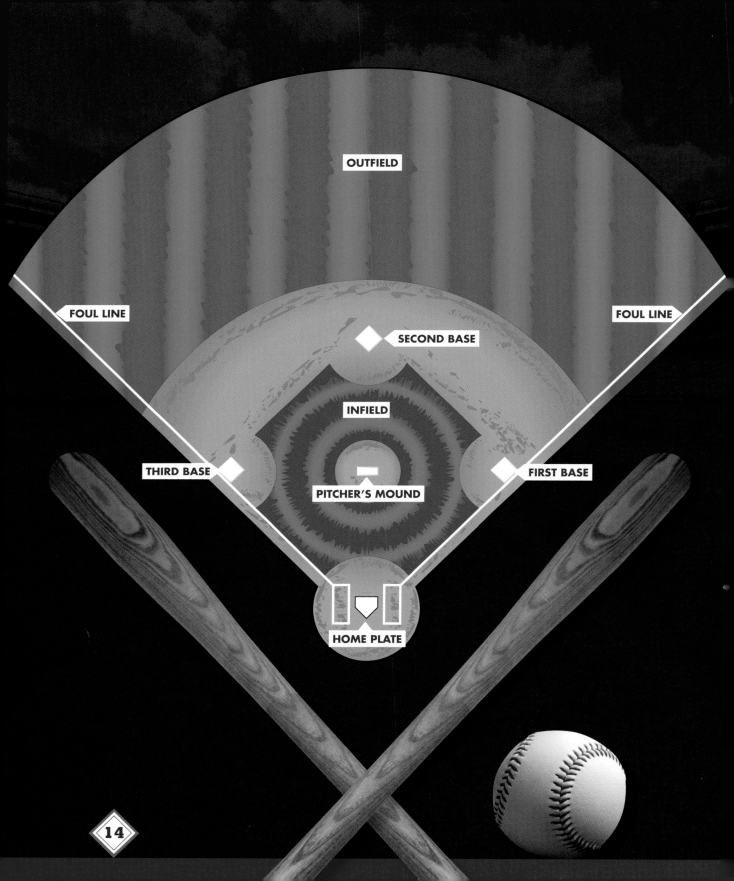

OUTFIELD

FOUL LINE

FOUL LINE

SECOND BASE

INFIELD

THIRD BASE

FIRST BASE

PITCHER'S MOUND

HOME PLATE

14

The Baseball Diamond

Baseball games are played on a diamond. Four bases form this diamond shape. The bases are 90 feet (27 m) apart. The area around the bases is called the **infield**. At the center of the infield is the pitcher's mound. The grass area beyond the bases is called the **outfield**. White lines start at home plate and go toward the outfield. These are the foul lines. Baseballs hit outside these lines are out of play. The outfield walls are about 300–450 feet (91–137 m) from home plate.

Big Days!

The Cardinals have had some great seasons in their long history. Here are three of the best:

1942: The Cardinals won the World Series this year. It was the first of three Series championships from 1942 to 1946.

1967: Thanks to Bob Gibson's great pitching, the Cardinals won another World Series. They beat the Boston Red Sox in a seven-game battle.

2006: St. Louis had the worst record of any team in the playoffs. But they won the World Series anyway! They beat the Chicago White Sox in five games.

Celebration time in St. Louis! The Cardinals poured onto the field ▶ after winning the 2006 World Series.

Tough Days!

The Cardinals have had more great seasons than almost any other team. But not every season can be a winner. Here are three of the worst:

1908: The Cardinals haven't had many really bad seasons. This was terrible, though. They lost 105 out of 154 games!

1990: The Cardinals finished last in their division. It hasn't happened again!

2005: The Cardinals lost in the playoffs for the fifth time in six seasons. The team's tough days ended in 2006, though. They won the World Series!

◄ Not even speedy Vince Coleman could avoid this tag during the Cardinals' tough 1990 season.

Meet the Fans

Cardinals fans are called the "smartest" in baseball. They know when to cheer for good plays by both teams. They also know when to let the Cardinals know they're not playing well! The seats look like a sea of red when the Cardinals play big games. Fredbird, the team **mascot**, helps the fans support their team!

A giant scoreboard helps fans track the action in Cardinals' games. ▶

Rogers Hornsby, Second Base

Heroes Then . . .

Second baseman Rogers Hornsby won two **Triple Crowns** and six N.L. batting titles. No player has topped his 1924 batting average of .424. Dizzy Dean was a goofy guy, but a great pitcher. He won 30 games in 1934. Outfielder Joe Medwick won a Triple Crown in 1937. Stan "The Man" Musial is the greatest all-time Cardinals player. He smacked an N.L.-record 3,630 hits from 1941 to 1963. Fireballing pitcher Bob Gibson was a World Series star, going 7–2 in three Series. Outfielder Lou Brock was one of baseball's best all-time base stealers. Ozzie Smith was the best-fielding shortstop ever. The "Wizard of Oz" dazzled fans with his glove work.

◀ Ozzie Smith (leaping) made his name with great **defense**. Inset: Rogers Hornsby was one of baseball's best hitters.

23

Heroes Now . . .

The Cardinals are proud to have today's best player. First baseman Albert Pujols amazes fans with his hitting ability. In voting for the **Most Valuable Player (MVP)**, Pujols has finished in the top four spots seven times. He has won two MVP awards . . . so far! He has played in eight All-Star Games and was the 2003 N.L. batting champ. The Cardinals' best pitcher is starter Chris Carpenter. He won the 2005 **Cy Young Award** as the N.L.'s top pitcher. He came back in 2009 from an arm injury. Catcher Yadier Molina was a 2009 All-Star. He is one of three Molina brothers to play catcher in the Majors.

Albert Pujols, First Base

Chris Carpenter, Pitcher

Yadier Molina, Catcher

BATTING HELMET

TEAM JERSEY

BATTING GLOVE

UNDERSHIRT

TEAM PANTS

CATCHER'S MASK

CHEST PROTECTOR

CATCHER'S MITT

BAT

CATCHER'S SHIN GUARD

BASEBALL CLEATS

Yadier Molina, Catcher

Gearing Up

Baseball players all wear a team jersey and pants. They have to wear a team hat in the field and a helmet when batting. Take a look at Skip Schumaker and Yadier Molina to see some other parts of a baseball player's uniform.

THE BASEBALL

A Major League baseball weighs about 5 ounces (142 g). It is 9 inches (23 cm) around. A leather cover surrounds hundreds of feet of string. That string is wound around a small center of rubber and cork.

SPORTS STATS

Here are some all-time career records for the St. Louis Cardinals. All the stats are through the 2009 season.

HOME RUNS

Stan Musial, 475
Albert Pujols, 366

RUNS BATTED IN

Stan Musial, 1,951
Enos Slaughter, 1,148

BATTING AVERAGE

Rogers Hornsby, .359
Johnny Mize, .336

WINS BY A PITCHER

Bob Gibson, 251

Jesse Haines, 210

STOLEN BASES

Lou Brock, 888

Vince Coleman, 549

WINS BY A MANAGER

Tony LaRussa, 1,232

EARNED RUN AVERAGE

Ed Karger, 2.46

John Tudor, 2.52

Glossary

All-Star Game a yearly game between the best players in each league

Cy Young Award an award given to the top pitcher in each league

defense when a team is in the field, trying to keep the other team from scoring

home plate a five-sided rubber pad where batters stand to swing, and where runners touch base to score runs

infield the area around and between the four bases of a baseball diamond

loyal supporting something no matter what

manager the person who is in charge of the team and chooses who will bat and pitch

mascot a person in costume or an animal that helps fans cheer for their team

Most Valuable Player (MVP) a yearly award given to the top player in each league

opponents teams or players that play against each other

outfield the large, grass area beyond the infield of a baseball diamond

rivals teams that play each other often and have an ongoing competition

Triple Crown leading a league in home runs, RBI, and batting average in the same season

World Series the Major League Baseball championship, played each year between the winners of the American and National Leagues

Find Out More

BOOKS

Buckley, James Jr. *Eyewitness Baseball*. New York: DK Publishing, 2010.

Christopher, Matt. *Albert Pujols*. New York: Little Brown Young Readers, 2009.

Stewart, Mark. *St. Louis Cardinals*. Chicago: Norwood House Press, 2008.

Teitelbaum, Michael. *Baseball*. Ann Arbor, MI: Cherry Lake Publishing, 2009.

WEB SITES

Visit our Web page for links about the St. Louis Cardinals and other pro baseball teams.

childsworld.com/links

Note to Parents, Teachers, and Librarians: We routinely verify our Web links to make sure they are safe, active sites—so encourage your readers to check them out!

FAVORITE BASEBALL TEAMS

Index

ABOUT THE AUTHOR

K.C. Kelley has written dozens of books on baseball and other sports for young readers. He has also been a youth baseball coach and called baseball games on the radio. His favorite team? The Boston Red Sox.